With love to our little angel, Zach
~ Mimi

THE WISE ANIMAL HANDBOOK

Kate B. Jerome

ARCADIA KIDS

Attempt new **skills** from **time** to **time**.

Just **try** to think them **through.**

And if you find you're left behind...

...then change your point of view.

Try not to think of just yourself.

Invent new ways to share.

Stay close to friends whom you can trust.

But
always
be
aware.

Avoid the tattle in the tale.

Insist that **truth** is **best.**

Embrace with **pride** the strengths you have.

Demand
to be
impressed.

Enjoy
the
peace
that
nature
brings.

Ignore what's just for show.

Join forces when the road gets rough.

Admit
when you
don't know.

Remember **family** is the **best.**

Despite the **ups** and **downs**.

Don't hide from things that you must face.

Make
joyful
laughing
sounds.

Eat
healthy
food to
grow
up
strong.

Be patient with your friends.

Try not to take a stubborn stand.

Be
quick
to make
amends.

Excuse
yourself
when
manners
slip.

Be **helpful** every **day.**

Keep trying even when it's hard.

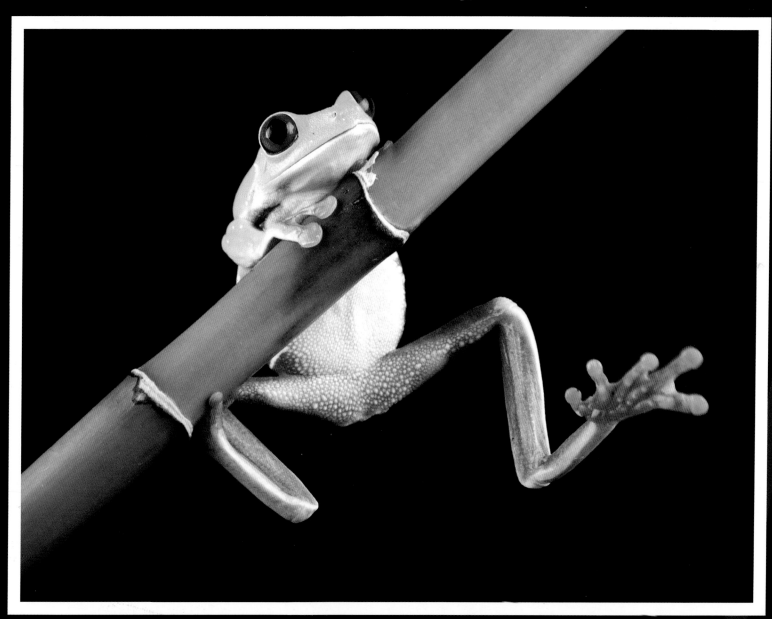

But
don't
forget to
play!

And
sing

...and **dance** each **day!**

Written by Kate B. Jerome
Design and Production: Lumina Datamatics, Inc.
Coloring Illustrations: Tom Pounders
Research: Eric Nyquist

Cover Images: See back cover

Interior Images: 002 Anetapics/Shutterstock.com; 003 George Green/Shutterstock.com; 004 Sergey Uryadnikov/Shutterstock.com; 005 Gnomeandi/Shutterstock.com; 006 Bruce MacQueen/Shutterstock.com; 007 Henk Bentlage/Shutterstock.com; 008 M.M./Shutterstock.com; 009 Mikael Damkier/Shutterstock.com; 010 Brendan van Son/Shutterstock.com; 011 Michael Pettigrew/Shutterstock.com; 012 StevenRussellSmithPhotos/Shutterstock.com; 013 Pakhnyushchy/Shutterstock.com; 014 Patjo/Shutterstock.com; 015 Quinn Martin/Shutterstock.com; 016 Lincoln Rogers/Shutterstock.com; 017 Dirk Ercken/Shutterstock.com; 018 Karel Gallas/Shutterstock.com; 019 Orangecrush/Shutterstock.com; 020 Guenter-foto/Shutterstock.com; 021 Janecat/Shutterstock.com; 022 Shironina/Shutterstock.com; 023 Annette Shaff/Shutterstock.com; 024 Vitaly Titov/Shutterstock.com; 025 Rohappy/Shutterstock.com; 026 MattiaATH/Shutterstock.com; 027 Otsphoto/Shutterstock.com; 028 FikMik/Shutterstock.com; 029 Four Oaks/Shutterstock.com; 030 Ekaterina Kolomeets/Shutterstock.com; 031 Hugh Lansdown/Shutterstock.com.

Published by Arcadia Kids, a division of Arcadia Publishing and
The History Press, Charleston, SC

For all general information contact Arcadia Publishing at:
Telephone: 843-853-2070
Email: sales@arcadiapublishing.com

For Customer Service and Orders:
Toll Free: 1-888-313-2665
Visit us on the Internet at www.arcadiapublishing.com

Library of Congress Cataloging-in-Publication data is on file with the publisher.

Printed in China